Everything is Love

POETRY FOR
All
OCCASIONS

by
Rev. Irene Danon

DEDICATION

This book is dedicated to all those who believe in a Higher Power.

Also, my daughters

Roberta

Laura

Michelle

Other books by Rev. Irene Danon

Failure is Not an Option,
Overcoming Obstacles with Faith
Prayer Treatments for all Occasions

Edited and Prepared for publication by
Rebecca Szetela

Cover Painting by Neill Oswald-Kuehn

Printed in the United States of America
Copyright 2014 by Rev. Irene Danon
ISBN-13 978-1500472535

All rights reserved, no part of this book may be reproduced or transmitted in any form or by any means, electronic or mechanical, including photographing, recording, or by any information storage and retrieval system, without the written permission of the publisher.

Rev. Irene Danon

Irene Danon grew up in Nazi occupied Yugoslavia as a frightened yet strong Jewish girl. Her courage, love of family and faith brought her through the war.

Irene and her family came to the United States as guests of president Roosevelt.

She loves this country and says the pledge of allegiance with pride.

This poetry book reflects some of her life experiences.

CONTENTS

	page
SCIENCE OF MIND	5
Praising God in Gratitude	7
There But For the Grace of God Go I	9
It's ok to Say No	11
Depression	12
The Gift	14
Healing 9/11 Why Me?	15
Outrageously Awesome	19
The Existentialist	21
Tomorrow May Not Be Soon Enough	22
Giving	23
Hazan	25
Perpetual and Eternal	26
PHILOSOPHY	27
Life	29
Not sure	30
Alcoholics Prayer	31
Forgiveness	32

CONTENTS

                                                                                                            Page

	Page
CHILD	35
Keeper of the Keys	37
Borrowed Coat	38
The Child	40
Blessing for the Child	41
To my Parents	43
War, Through The Eyes of a Child	44
My Child	46
DEATH	47
The End or a Beginning	49
When You Die - *Laura Danon*	51
I Was Not Ready	53
So Long My Friend	54
Release	56
Realization of Loss	58
Fever	60
Yesterday's Music	61
He Mended Wooden Hearts - *Roberta Danon*	62

CONTENTS

Page

ALL ABOUT LOVE 65

    What is Love (contemporary) 67

    Take My Hand (Wedding vow) 68

    Balance of Power 69

    Do not Fear 71

    You and Me, etc. 72

    Lost Dream 73

    Mr. Hamid 74

    Renaissance of Peace 75

    Love (S O M style) 76

    Do I dare at 50 77

    Ode to an Impatient Man 78

    Because you Loved Me 79

    May You 81

JEWISH THEMES 83

    On Becoming a Jew 85

    Dark Images 86

    Jewish Pain 87

CONTENTS

JEWISH THEMES (continued)

page

I Stand Alone 88

What is a Jew 89

Rebirth 91

For Rabbi Nina 93

Never Forget 94

OTHER 97

Hurricane 99

Letting Go 101

Don't You Know - *Michelle Danon* 103

PETS 105

Blessing a Pet 107

Healing the Passing of Emily, Our Pet 108

WAR 111

Peace From Within 113

Agony of war 115

Defenders of Freedom 116

SCIENCE OF MIND

PRAISING GOD IN GRATITUDE

O Divine Spirit!
How I love to feel
your energy enveloping,
loving and expressing
yourself through me.

I feel this magnificent exuberance.
I feel that I can stretch my arms
and embrace the entire world.

Yet it is Your spiritual arms
that reach through me
and allow me to help,
to touch, to heal, and love.

My Beloved,
You have endowed me
with such graces
and made my life
so very beautiful and rich.
You have given me sight.
You have given me senses
To feel, to smell, and to touch.

You have given me a mind
To exercise my will and make decisions.

You have created me in your own image,
Giving me perfection of body and soul.
You have given me heart
Full of endless self-generating love
That will never spend itself;
But grow richer each time, I use it.

You, My God, ARE THE MAGNIFICENCE!
You are the Power! You are the Energy!
You are, the air I breath, the life I live.
You are the energy which gave rise to my soul.
You, my Beloved, are me in Flesh,
For which I am eternally grateful.

THERE BUT FOR
THE GRACE OF GOD GO I

She lay in the doorway.
Her body twisted, cold, messy.
She lost a shoe,
exposing a hole in her sock,
with her dirty toe peering out.

The glasses on her face, are bent.
What does she see?
What does she feel?
Does she feel at all?
Is her life so painful
that she shut off her feelings?

Perhaps she is dreaming
of the family she once had,
the home, and the warm bed
she slept in?
Her children who deny her
and the reality of her aloneness.

Her pain and her sorrow,
parts of the map
on her weather- beaten face.
Her hair matted and dirty,
while a few gray hairs frame her soul
and give it substance.

I looked at her.
My guts wrenched with pain of empathy.
What if I had been born to her mother,
and she to mine?
Would it, could it,
Could this be me?

THERE BUT,
FOR THE GRACE OF GOD GO I !

IT'S OK TO SAY NO

I couldn't say no,
Even if it hurt me.
I couldn't say no
Even it hurt them.

I gave my children all.
I took away their pain.
I took away their tears.
I took away their growth.

I couldn't say no to a friend.
Even if it hurt me.
I couldn't say no to a stranger,
Even though it wasn't helping.

Then I got my faith and felt God.
I gave up my ego,
And learned to say no.
I trusted and walked away.

The universe knows,
Divine Mind guides,
God decides,
And I respect myself.

DEPRESSION

From the depth of the
  Caverns of my mind,
Depression lurks,
  Waiting to attack.

I push it back,
  And turn on the TV.
For a while,
  I win.

It returns, with a passion,
  Stronger and darker.
I pick up a book,
  Listen to music, I eat.

The panic grows
  Heavier and grayer.
And I am getting
  Weaker and darker.

Like a boa envelops its prey,
  It wraps itself around me,
Choking me,
  Killing my desire to resist.

Tears, my only weapon, flow freely.
  My body spent.
My mind suspended in inertia
  As I give up to sleep.

But tomorrow
  Is another day.
And I wake up
  With God.

My feet touch the ground.
  My mind is made up.
I let go and let God.
  I found my weapon.

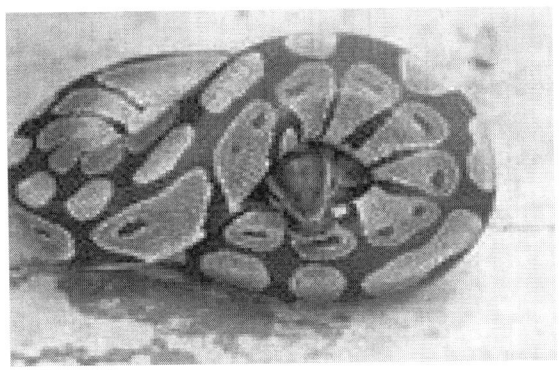

THE GIFT

How can I give to you
that which you already have?
How can I recognize for you
that which God has already done?

I can only be for you
an instrument of God.
I can only remind you
that you are an expression of God.

So my only gift to you
can be an awareness
that whatever you can conceive,
you can achieve.

HEALING---------- 9/11/01
WHY ME?

Why was I saved when so many perished?
Why was my life spared and brought to this point in time?
Was there a job for me to do?

Like Jacob, who wrestled with the angel all night,
so do I wrestle with this thought constantly.
And then I start questioning
the existence of God
and my relationship to Him.
So many questions fill my consciousness
that the search for answers becomes an obsession.

Each time I ask myself
"what do I feel?"
The tears flood my eyes
and a heavy sadness envelops me.

Where did they all go?
Where are they now?
All those multitudes of souls
whose lives appear
to have been taken away from them prematurely.
Is there a life after death?
Are their souls on the way to further development
or was this just an abrupt ending;

like turning the on and off switch to off
leaving behind mothers crying for the parts of
themselves to which they gave birth?
Little children,
questioning, not understanding.
Why isn't my daddy coming home?

Why was my life spared?
I ask again.
What can I do to ease this pain,
and satisfy this answer?
How can I serve you, my God,
when I don't understand?
When I don't know what You want me to do.

I can write checks,
and share that which you have given me.
I can be charitable in my heart,
and forgive, those who hurt me.
I can spread my love,
like a blanket,
across each person I touch,
and ease their pain.
I can pray to You,
and ask Your forgiveness
for ever doubting you.
Or,

I can pull myself together,
wipe the tears from my eyes,
erase the pain from my heart and know
that you, Divine spirit, have a plan for me.
I can Trust.
I can work and rebuild my faith
and know that Spirit,
that essence of life never dies.

That my soul, and the souls of all beings,
never stop,
that the souls began when You,
my Beloved, blew the breath of life into us,
and that it will never end,
because You my God,
are eternal and forever,
and we are one with You.

So I continue peacefully
on my journey to eternity,
trusting in Your infinite Power and Wisdom .
Knowing that I don't know,
but never losing my faith,
and continuing to serve You,
My God, by loving my fellow men,
by being just and fair and moral,
because when I love,
I afford You, my beloved,
a vehicle to express Yourself.

And then I realize, that
YOU SAVED ME,
SO THAT YOU CAN EXPRESS
YOUR LOVE THROUGH ME.
And I am so grateful and honored to be

an expression of You, in human form.

OUTRAGEOUSLY AWESOME

Many moons ago,
before my soul was clothed in this body,
I was free.
Free to soar the heights of the Divine.
I danced with angels and rejoiced with God.

But two earthlings
were sad, for they wanted
someone to love.
So God asked me
to go and fill their hearts.

And I did. And I descended
into the belly of the human.
They loved me and cared for me
and they thought
I belong to them.

But my body was there only
to fill their human needs.
And I was there to love them
and to fill my human needs.
For I too, became a mortal.

And my soul forgot my path,
for my humanness took over.
But the Spirit in me still knew.
It loved and it shared
and it expressed the essence of God.

Most years were good
and some were hard.
And the body showed the wear.
But the soul remained forever young
and looked forward to going home.

Now I return to my fathers' mansion
with a mixture of feelings.
Sadness to leave and joy to return.
And when I am asked, how was it?
I reply OUTRAGEOUSLY AWESOME.

THE EXISTENTIALIST

Prisoner of your mind
Stuck in your skin.
The fear of failure
Holds you in.

There is no failure
There is no fate
Only a wall
With an open gate.

Break the shell
And crack the spree
Reach for the stars
And you'll feel free.

TOMORROW MAY NOT
BE SOON ENOUGH

How many times
 in life, we wish
  We had done this, or that.

How many times
 we wish we had
  Acted instead of waited?

How hard it is
 to look in the mirror
  And know time is passing?

So take heed
 my friend and do
  What you want to do today.

For life's fragile fragrance
 will quickly fade away,
  And leave you longing.

So take charge, take your power
 and act now, for tomorrow
  May not be soon enough.

GIVING

Do you water the flowers
  after the rain?
Do you feed the animals
  after they have eaten
And wonder why they don't eat?

Do you give umbrellas
  on a beautiful day?
Do you give suntan lotion
  on a cloudy day
And think how ungrateful people are?

Do you give your love
  when one needs it?
Or do you give it
  when one is not in the mood.
And then you get angry?

Do you give to others
  when and what they need?
Or do you give
  when you want
And what you feel they should have?

To give when you wish and what you want,
  is hardly giving at all.
For it derives from selfish,
  ego satisfying motives.
And it only satisfies the giver
  and not the receiver.

Giving without
  having others applaud you
Is unselfish giving.

But the sincerest giving of all is
  giving to the one who needs
what he wants
  and when he needs it
without being asked,
  even if you have to give up
what you love dearly.

But most of all,
  never expecting to be paid back.

HAZAN

There was a fellow named Hazan
And a magic rug had he.
From oasis to oasis
He would fly with whim and glee.

With his lips of love he whispered
To the water and the tree
It appeared that he was happy
But inside, lonely was he.

Wasteland desert little gave him
So he sought the food for mind.
But one thing he failed to notice,
First himself he had to find.

PERPETUAL AND ETERNAL
(The cycle of life)

When sun's last rays fade away
Like the embers of a burning fire,
And the child is put to rest
The night is born.

Like black magic with its wonder,
It gives refuge to the haunted,
Hugs the lover and hides the thief
And the night lives on.

But darkness, which seemed eternal
Used its youth and spent its vigor
Now gives way to a yearning day
For the night is dying.

PHILOSOPHY

LIFE

An unfinished symphony,
A fragile, filament of reason,
A ray of sunshine, an eagles flight.
The end of the rainbow.

Is our blessing
In the ignorance
Of the final stroke?

Or do we sail along
In the bliss
Of unawareness?

What would
We change if
We didn't feel immortal?

Would we live differently?
Would we be kinder, more giving,
More considerate and honest?

Is this universe so vast
Making us incapable
Of comprehending the whole?
Or,

Are we simply
A self destructing fiber
In the tapestry of essence?

NOT SURE

Like the wounded antelope,
Your ego cries with pain.
The pain inflicted upon you
Not by environment, but by
Internal unrest.

It cries in search of an answer.
What is this madness we call life?
What are the exquisite experiences?
Are they realities or figments of our imagination?

But you find no answers.
For how can you find
An answer to life,
If you aren't even sure
Of your existence?

ALCOHOLICS' PRAYER

Holy Spirit, God,
Protect my mind.
Guide my hands
Stay with me
In the time of my craving.

I don't want to die.
I don't want to fall.
I don't want to drink.
Guide me, my God
Infuse me with Your strength.

I know what the bottom is.
I hit it once.
I know what the pain is.
I felt it often.
Hold my hand, O God.

When I am with you,
I am strong.
When I have faith
I know who I am
And I am grateful.

FORGIVENESS

Anger and revenge are poisons
Which eat up your body
Like cancer.
Forgiveness is the antidote.

Forgiveness is a gift to YOU.
Forgiveness tears down the
Prison bars of hate and sets you free.
It helps you move on.

Forgive yourself.
Your errors were lessons.
Love yourself, and know
God has already forgiven you.

Forgive them before they die.
For when they are gone.
It is the end and you can never.
Call them to say, "I love you!"

When you are controlled by anger
You suffer, you hurt, you ail.
While the person you are angry with
Doesn't even know you exist.

Take control of your life.
Breathe in love,
Breathe out hate.
Bless those who hurt you.

Forgive them in your heart.
Release them in your mind.
Heal yourself.
Move on and feel

CHILD

"Keeper of the Keys" Artwork by Linda Jarvis

KEEPER OF THE KEYS

Dedicated to my daughter Roberta
The piano tuner

You are the keeper of the keys.
With your hands and your ears
You give a special meaning to music.
You create the perfection of sound.
You feed the soul with love.
You tantalize the senses with the sound of God.
He has created you so He can
express perfection of sound through your hands.

So keep on, my little keeper of the keys
And make the world a better place.
And with the sound of perfect pitch
Raise the world
From sadness to joy.
From darkness to light.
From disharmony to harmony.

YOU ARE ONE WITH YOUR CREATOR.

BORROWED COAT
(from daughter)

Yesterday I borrowed your coat.
I felt your little arms and soft hair
Spill all over me,
And keep me warm.

Yesterday, when you were born,
You were the light of my life.
You were my reason for living.
You were my gift from God.

And then you grew up.
Together at the past we gazed
And the errors I made.
With limited knowledge, you judged me.

For years I atoned,
But only in vain.
For the harder I tried,
The more you condemned me.

Through many tears of pain
I severed the strings.
Through prayer, I forgave myself.
I let you go, and left you to God.

Yesterday I borrowed the coat
From my little girl,
And today, I returned it
To my dearest friend.

THE CHILD

A child is our
Gift from God
Who chose us to be
His parents.

But God
Wanted us only
To be the child's
Temporary guardians.

So let's enjoy
The love and the warmth
That he or she brings
And let's show
The child the way back to God.

BLESSING FOR THE CHILD

Beloved spirit! I know
That I am one with you!
I know that I am
An expression of you.
I know that I am
God expression in human form.

I am so grateful, beloved spirit
That you have chosen me
To be your instrument
And bring into the world
This beautiful creature,
I call my child.
I am filled with awe
And gratitude for this miracle.

The perfect little body,
The tiny fingers,
The rosebud mouth, the soul,
The heart and the mind
Through which
You express yourself
Again and again and again.
Everlasting and eternal.

I am grateful
To be the keeper
Of this special bundle.
I know that I am worth
Of your trust.

I know that you express
Your wisdom, Your love
And eternity through
This precious little being.

And when things appear
To get out of hand
And challenges fill the air
Around us, I know, Beloved Spirit
That you are always here.

And when I feel helpless,
I know that you are here.
And when things appear darkest,
You are here guiding and protecting.
So in spite of appearance, I trust.

I release this most precious possession to You.
Because it is You.
It is the essence of You God.
I am filled with gratitude,
Love and faith.
I know that our child is always safe,
And protected.
Now I release our child
Totally to You
With full confidence and knowing
That my child is You,
And you are glorious, my beloved.

TO MY PARENTS

There are riches in this world
that one can have and hold.
But there is nothing I'd have rather
then my only mother and father.

Some like heavens so high and blue,
others like the morning dew,
but I don't care for natures fad
I just love my mother and dad.

When I'm in trouble and need a hand,
always by me they'll stand
With love and help they'll come,
my wonderful dad and mom.

Thanks dear parents for all you've done.
Although sometimes it hasn't been fun.
For me you hold that magic touch.
That's why I love you so much.

WAR-
THROUGH THE EYES OF A CHILD

What is happening, Daddy?
I am scared of bombs.
Is someone trying to kill us, daddy?
The noise is awful.

Is our house going to
fall on us and burry us?
They don't even know us.
Was I a bad girl, daddy?
I promise, I will be good.

Why do people hate us, daddy?
They don't even know us!
Make them go away.
I am very scared, daddy.

They stopped. The noise stopped.
Can I go out and play?
I can't breath. I am choking.
The air is so dusty.
Look daddy, there is a hand.... and a leg....
Where is the person, daddy?

Are you afraid, daddy?
Are you scared we are going to die?
Is God taking a nap?
You said God will take care of us.
You promised. You promised.
Where is God, daddy?

MY CHILD

One day, I looked at your father
and said, I want another baby.
Your father took me by the hand,
into the bedroom and you evolved
from ethereal to material.

And your body was conceived inside my body.
And my cells became your cells.
And you grew inside my belly.
And when I was ready to release
your body into this world,
God blew His breath of life into you
and you gave a cry of joy;
for you experienced your first breath.

Growing up was hard,
But He was there with you.
Even when you didn't know or believe,
He was there with you.
Now that you have evolved
Into this beautiful butterfly
you recognize and see Him
in every step. You know Him,
Because you are Him in human flesh.

DEATH

THE END OR THE BEGINNING

How many of us fear death,
and think of it as just an end?
How many of us think of death
as a painful experience?

Today, when a person faces death,
many people think it is the end.
But how can we be sure
that this is not just another beginning?
A graduation to a higher level of existence?

A human being is a SOUL
clothed in a body.
This body, this vessel that we acquire at birth,
is the human part of us.
It is the Spirit within us
which is Eternal and everlasting.
It is the part of us that always was
and forever will be, because
It is the Part of us which is God.

When the body reaches
the end of its process, we release it.
We shed it like a snake sheds its skin.
The soul looks forward to a higher plane
and death becomes relief,
and not a painful experience.
Yet it is not the fear of death, but
the quality of life that is of concern on this plane.

Our spirit or energy is what we leave
after the body is gone.
Our love is what we disseminate and share
during our lifetime.
And our legacy is what we leave to the world
to be remembered by.

WHEN YOU DIE
By Laura Danon

When you die

your spirit leaves your body.

It becomes part of the greater

"Ebb and Flow" of life

It becomes the breath in

and the breath out.

It becomes the wave

as it lingers on the sand

and leaves it's foamy remnants behind.

It becomes one with the wind

as it rushes through the trees,

or a hurricane,

or a soft breeze,

as it gently caresses someone's skin.

When you die,

your Spirit becomes one with it all.

You bend and flow and ride

the vibrations of the Earth,

the thermal in the sky

and the waves of the Sea.

You become one with the deep

hues of the orange sunset,

and the rich, fertile,

brown soil of the earth.

Because that Spirit that you are, never dies.

It continues on to occupy other vessels,

in other spaces, never forgetting

the magnificence of who you are.

I WAS NOT READY

Yesterday, I met death.
But I wasn't afraid,
For I didn't recognize it.

It seemed gentle
And it seemed kind
As it touched my hand.

There was light
And there was peace.
But I wasn't ready.

We'll meet again
My friend
And I may welcome you

But today,
I feel wonderful.
So I bid you, so long.

SO LONG MY FRIEND
Dedicated to the memory of Rick Davidson

Through the shadows
Of life gone by
I still see you
And feel you.

You were the gentle soul.
You were the spring.
You came into my life
To help me blossom.

But my winter was strong.
Ice was everywhere.
Darkness and fear
Were all I knew.

With your warmth and honesty,
You brought love.
You gave to me
And you gave to my girls.

You gave us art.
You gave us freedom.
You gave us truth.
You called me beautiful.

So this is not goodby,
But only so long, my friend.
For YOU shall LIVE in our hearts
Until we meet again.

RELEASE
Dedicated to my brother Ike

Release my weakened body,
And give flight to my soul.
I have lived and I have loved,
And now it's time for me to go.

I have laughed and I have cried
And I have lived well.
I've helped others,
And served you, my God.

I've seen the miracle of life, (birth)
And I've seen the cruelty of men.
I beg forgiveness, if I hurt you
And I forgive the hurts toward me.

Please, release this body
For it served me well.
But this is the end
And I must go home.

No more pain...
No more agony...
No more problems...
Regained dignity...

I embrace You, my beloved.
I give thanks for my gift of life.
It was not wasted...
I feel Your presence...

I see Your outstretched arms.
I am safe...
Serenity....
Peace at last...

THE REALIZATION OF LOSS

And when the last shovel of earth,
Descends upon the coffin,
And it is lowered into the womb of mother earth,
A part of you goes with it.

First comes the numbness.
For the pain is so great
That it anaesthetizes you,
And ties you up in knots.

You can't think, you don't feel.
You just act and react.
You shake hands, you talk
And you move your body, automatically.

Then the crowd leaves,
And the quiet, fills all the crevices
And corners of your mind.
Vacuum becomes louder than thunder.

The anger starts tearing into you.
The fury and questioning of God.
Hows and whys keep spinning,
While you want to strike.

(To God)You don't care about your creation!
You don't care about me!
You don't care about anybody!
I am not even sure you exist.

But the beauty and love
The sunshine, which his spirit still is
Fills you, embraces you, reaches out to you,
And you know, it is everlasting and eternal.

That which is, can never die.
His smile, his legacy, his love,
The memories, the sharing,
Will always be with you and a part of you.

And then with light upon your face,
And gratitude in your heart
You give thanks for experiencing
And sharing the preciousness which he was.

FEVER

Oh sweet eternity!
Extend your arms to me.
Reach out and take my hand.

Cast your shadow and protect me
From the burning sun.
Cool off my lips with your kiss,
And rub my back with your icy fingertips.

Let me rest my head on your shoulder
Let me be one with you.
O' please, give me that eternal peace.

YESTERDAY'S MUSIC

The music goes on,
and my head goes into a spin.
My soul melts into days of long ago.

My heart cries
with joy and pain of yesterdays memories,
when the world was young
and the grass was green
and my body was strong.
And love and excitement
were bursting forth from my entire being.

But now is the autumn of my years.
And the grass is turning brown.
And the leaves are wilting and falling,
but the song still echoes
in my head and in my heart.

So I go to sleep with a smile on my face
because my soul will never age or die,
and the music,
like the Divine Universe, will never cease.

HE MENDED WOODEN HEARTS
Memorial for Larry Brown
by Roberta Danon

Went to Brownie's house today
Had something on my mind
Needed to remember times
When life seemed much more kind

He mended wooden hearts with strings
Antique angels bowed with wings
Sad little children, how he did adore
Sitting, standing, lined up waiting
There on Larry's floor

I went back and ran upstairs
But something felt different from before
There was a sign taped to the wall
Said, "Closed, For Evermore"

Oh Brownie, Oh Oh Brownie
Brownie, where did you go?
Are you mining in the Zonies
or fishing in the snow?

Oh Brownie my friend Brownie,
How I miss your curly hair
Across the bridge, over the rainbow,
Is there music everywhere?

He had the way of making things
So much better than before
Ah... to be a wooden child
In line on Brownie's floor.

ALL ABOUT LOVE

WHAT IS LOVE

Love is death
For to love is to die a little.
Love is sadness,
For to love is to suffer.
Love is giving,
For to love is to give of yourself
Love is exhausting
For it makes you ascend and descend
different planes of consciousness.
Love is stimulating
For it gives you vigor
you never thought you had.
Love is cruel
For it leaves you vulnerable.
Love is ambiguous
For it makes you want and refuse
At the same time.
Love is a paradox
For it makes you say no when you mean yes.
Love is nuts
So I'll leave it to the squirrels!

TAKE MY HAND
A wedding vow

Take my hand
And walk this road with me.
There will be smooth paths
And there will be uphill climbs.

And we will support each other
Every step of the way.
Yet I will walk in my shoes
And you in yours.

I won't try to change you,
But I will accept you, as you are.
And I know, that our love is strong enough
That you can do the same.

So take my hand
And share this gift of life with me.
Be my soul mate on this plane
And let our spirits soar
To the new heights of the divine.

BALANCE OF POWER

The willow stood
tall and graceful
strong, unyielding
to the wind and the sun.

The king of the garden
towering over
and shading fully
the flora beneath.

Next to it, a rose,
delicate, pale and scented
with thorns sharp,
longing for warmth of the sun.

But the willow,
was tall, with branches
wide and strong,
shading the rose.

At midnight, the hurricane.
It tore and uprooted,
Broke the willow's branches.
And twisted the rose.

In the morning, the willow was sad.
Its strength was depleted
And the rose felt roasted
From the glaring sun.

The willow reigns again;
but its branches are shorter,
And the rose blooms profusely.
For it learned to enjoy the sun.

Peace and harmony
emanate in my garden now.
For the willow so strong,
complements the delicate rose.

DO NOT FEAR

Do not fear, dear love,
That I'll reveal
Those hours of pleasure
We two have stolen.

No eye shall see
Nor yet the sun decree
What you and I
Have done.

No ear shall hear our love
Yet we, silent
As the night
Shall be.

The God of love himself
Whose dart did
First wound mine,
And then your heart

Shall never know,
That we can tell
What sweetness
In stolen embraces dwell.

YOU AND ME, ETC...

The first quarrel had occurred,
angrily the words did race.
The first pain had stabbed her heart
and the first tear had marred her face.

The second round should be better,
they tell us and contend,
for we are weary and much smarter
if we're honest and don't pretend.

But WE ARE a total package
of our experiences we are the sum.
The good things and the bad ones
we deliver on our drum.

"Twas not with you, that I was angry",
he mumbled aghast,
"I too could not, my own self contain",
she sobbed, revealing her past

Like Dr. Pavlov's, animals we are,
and can explode like a shell,
for our past is full of anger,
which is brought out by the bell.

THE LOST DREAM

A dream that vanished into nowhere
A dream that really was
A dream as real as you and I
A dream that you were close.

But it wasn't all a dream;
For I was not asleep.
I had loved you and caressed you
And felt emotion deep.

You taught me to be a lover.
You awakened the woman in me.
I had loved you, really loved you;
But some things are not meant to be.

TO MR. HAMID, MY FRIEND

My fairy tale Prince.
His kindly manner.
His gentle voice.
He flies on his magic rug.

He is the essence
Of all the oils of Arabia.
He is the song of
The Desert of Iran.

He loves the Koran,
He trusts his God.
His soul blossoms with love
His energy comes from above.

His consciousness high,
His mind is free.
He enjoys it all
With all humanity.

RENAISSANCE OF PEACE
For Abused Women

Like a bill collector,
Death has come for its own.
That final stroke,
That final breath.

No more waiting rooms
In the chamber of the mind.
No more amputations
Of self esteem, and dignity.

No more angry, frustrating,
Self destructing eating binges,
No more wasted tears and
Unappreciated sacrifices.

Only the absence remains.
The absence of sadistic emotional abuse.
The absence of tearing of egos.
The absence of defending.

Defending your views, your integrity.
The absence of fighting for survival,
The absence of pain.
And only the renaissance of peace remains.

LOVE
SCIENCE OF MIND STYLE

Love is the most powerful
healing energy in the universe.

Love is, what makes you
spur on and push forward.

Love is what makes babies grow
and puppies thrive.

Love is what makes a man
feel like a man.

Love is what makes
a woman blossom.

Love heals the sick.
And gives courage to the weak.

Love is :
GOD EXPRESSION IN HUMAN FORM

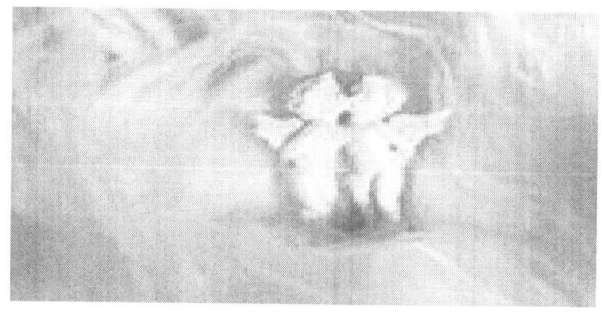

DO I DARE AT 50

Do I dare,
let the thoughts of you
permeate my whole being
and make me tremble
like a teenager?

Do I dare,
dream the dreams
of tomorrow
and fill myself with the fantasies
of the future

Do I dare
touch your face
with my fingertips
and kiss your
sad eyes?

Do I dare
make you smile
watch you laugh?
bring you happiness
and give you joy
Do I dare
love you?

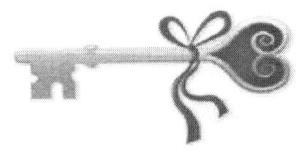

ODE TO AN IMPATIENT MAN

At the end of every rainbow
There's a shiny pot of gold.
With its riches it attracts you.
Whether you are young or old.

But the trip across that rainbow
Is so lengthy, hard and slow
For the colors are just tightropes
And across them you must go.

And as you look across that rainbow
And are blinded by the light
You see nothing but the riches
And accelerate your flight.

Consequently while rushing,
Your balance you do lose.
And between the hopes you tangle
Frustrated, swearing at the noose.
So,

Whatever your pot of gold is
Never rush in with a rage.
Take it gently and be patient
Because reward is for the sage!

BECAUSE YOU LOVED ME
To Donna Candiotti

Goodby, beautiful lady.
You lived, you loved
You paid your dues
And left a legacy.

You knew pain,
And you knew sorrow.
You lived with joy
And died in peace.

You were the bridge,
The hope and life,
Between the old world
And the new.

From Turkey,
Across the sea
To the States
You came to be.

You worshiped your God,
With a smile on you face.
Your kindness was real
For the whole human race.

Your "burekas y juevos"
Were a wonderful treat.
When after the temple,
At your home, we did meet.

"Fijika mia" you used to call me,
So in my heart for ever you'll be.
My own life is now richer
"Querida Donna", because you loved me.

MAY YOU

May each of you fill
With the essence of other.
May you share every sunrise
And every sunset together.

May your life be filled
With Gods' love, rainbows, and song.
May you learn, give,
And take from each other.

May you walk side by side,
And lean on each other.
May you exchange your dreams,
Fantasies, passions, and nightmares.

May you grow old together,
And share the rest of your life
With each other.

JEWISH THEME

ON BECOMING A JEW

When did I a Jew become?
When did I consent?
When did I rejections accept,
When was my spirit bent.

I am a jew
And I know fear.
I was in hiding
Just yesteryear.

Barbed wires and yellow stars
Were our only sight.
Broken spirits as well as bodies,
And we couldn't fight.

The price was dear,
And pain was deep,
The loss was huge,
And I did weep.

For Israel I thank God today,
And start my life anew.
I am proud of the fact
That I was born a Jew.

DARK IMAGES
(of a survivor)

Dark images
Run through my mind
Twisted and distorted
Vivid yet blind.

Some are anger
And some are fear,
Some are the relatives,
I used to hold dear.

I feel the pain
As I watch the shapes,
Some are bent
And some are just capes.

What do I do,
To ease this pain
What do I do
Not to go insane.

JEWISH PAIN

You walk, you talk,
You play, and you run.
And as the tired sun reclines,
The twilight in your mind is born.

Jungs' collective consciousness
Dominates your psyche.
You are a jew.
You suffer, you agonize.

The pain gnaws at you.
It makes you bleed.
This not only the pain of today,
But centuries of Jewish torment.

You survived, but the guilt lingers on.
Your helpless body tosses and turns.
Then soaked with tears, relief and gratitude,
You welcome another day.

I STAND ALONE

I stand alone.
Yesterday they were all here.
Today they are all Dead.
They are all dead and gone.

Slaughtered, gassed,
burned and buried.
Why did I survive?
What did God want me to do?

What is the purpose for my life?
How can I serve Him?
And why did He
Allow this to happen?

He did nothing.
He said nothing.
He just cried
In pain for his creation.

WHAT IS A JEW

What is a Jew?
Can anybody just say
"I am a Jew"
And become one?
Who is a Jew?

A little boy? A little girl?
A grown man? A woman?
A butcher, a doctor, a cop?
A banker, a thief, a stockbroker?

Perhaps all of the above, plus a lot more.
For to be a Jew is to feel in the underground
Passages of your mind the pain of millions
Of Jews who have suffered than perished.

To be a Jew is to have cried a thousand tears
And saved the unshed ones for tomorrow.

To be a Jew is to have
The unconscious collective memories of
The burning of Temples,
The Ghettos, the Spanish Inquisition, Dachau
And Treblinka.

To be a Jew is to cherish your family more
Than your own life.
To be a Jew is to make sacrifices
For your children, and tell them so.

To be a Jew is to feel guilty.
To be a Jew is to love chicken soup,
Made by a Yiddish Mamme.

To be a Jew is to give to charities,
Until it hurts.

But most of all, to be a Jew,
Is to eat a corned beef sandwich
On Jewish rye with mustard,
Instead of white bread with mayonnaise.

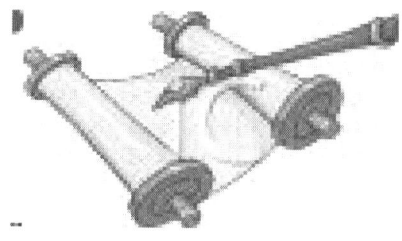

RE-BIRTH

I was born a Jew
Then Hitler came.
I hid. I lied. I stole.
But mostly,
I denied my Jewish Heritage.

I lived as Greek Orthodox.
I lived as Catholic.
The Jew in me went dormant
and I denied
the existence of God.

Here in this holy Temple
With Rabbi Bouskila,
With his classes,
His love and patience,
The Jew in me awakened.
The Jew that God created
And wanted to survive.

I know that,
That which God gave to me,
Such as the will to live,
Integrity, compassion
And the Jew in me, will never die.
Because I am that I am.
I am an expression and love of God.
I am a Jew.

And because of this holy place,
I am proud and unafraid
To celebrate my Bat-Mitzvah
And my rebirth as a Jew.

Irene Danon was Bat- Mitzvah at age 65 at the Temple Tifereth Israel of Los Angeles

FOR RABBI NINA

You are a Rabbi now.
You are a vehicle for God.
God had put you on this earth
To honor Him.

God had given you this life
So you can teach others
To express love, peace
Harmony and unity.

You are now a vessel for God.
You are the guiding light.
You are the expression of God
In human form.

And when your mother conceived you
And gave you life, she did n't know
She would be blessing us
With your divine presence now.

NEVER FORGET

Let's take our power back.
Let's not complain about the past.
But let us be strong
And united now.

Let us show Iran
And France, and the England
That we have been around
For 5667 years.

Let us show the world
That Moses, Ruth and Abraham
Still live within
Each and every one of us.

Let us show the Moslems,
That we are not afraid
For we know
That God is still with us.

So let's build up
Our land, Israel.
Let's plant the trees
And make the desert boom.

Let us show God
That His faith and love
For us
Have not been wasted.

Hadasah Hospital, Jerusalem

OTHER

THE HURRICANE
ESTER, LORA, RUTH

She comes out of nowhere
Tiptoeing softly through the night.
She whispers to the trees
And sings with the birds.

She dances, whirls and sways
Bewitching and bewildering her prey
Till hopelessly and helplessly
Despising her they fall at her feet.

Forsaken and seeking revenge
Untamed with passionate rage
She bedevils, confuses and uproots
Everything in her path.

And when she spends herself
She lowers her head in shame.
Disgust and contempt swell her bosom
While her eyes flood with tears.

Then all is still.
The night is over
A new day begins
And she returns to her nowhere.

LETTING GO

Your body achy and tout.
Too much exercise too many weights.
Your muscles ache with pain and desire.
You recline on the massage table
And close your eyes.

A soft towel
Covers your breasts
And the essence of you.
The light is dim
And the sounds of Mozart
Permeate the room.

He touches your shoulders.
You take a deep breath
And relax. His fingers
Slide up and down your neck.
You take another deep breath
And the music disappears.

His hands encompass your
Arms and your shoulders
And make your blood flow.
His palms, laden with lush emulsion
Slush across your abdomen,
And stimulate your internal organs.

Your muscles
Scream in silence,
Then yield to fervent passion
As you totally let go.
The soft moaning sounds
Roll off your lips.

He makes his way
To your calves and your feet.
The firmness of his touch
Leaves you open and vulnerable
He rubs your thighs,
He rubs your buttocks.

The table on which you recline disappears.
You float suspended in space.
There is no room. There is no towel.
There is no you.
Only the touch of his hands
Remains in your consciousness.

DON'T YOU KNOW
YOUR LIGHT IS SHINING?

By Michelle Danon
Singer/ Song writer

Look at me, don't turn away.
It's time you heard the truth.
You think you lost that specialness
that only comes with youth.
They tell you, you're not good enough.

But it's all a bed of lies.
Don't you know your light is shining
      And I can see it in your eyes.

We've all been to that scary place
where pain is all you feel.
A minute seems to never end
You're spinning on a wheel.
Those things that try to break you
are only lessons in disguise.
Don't you know your light is shining
      And I can see it in your eyes.

Sometimes it seems we're all alone
without a master plan,
but in the silence rings the truth,
the Spirit of I Am.

God's love will warm and hold you
with a flame that never dies
Don't you know you light is shining,
     And I can see it in your eyes.

Shine, shine, shine, for me,
Shine, shine, let yourself be the Light

PETS

BLESSING A PET

Beloved Spirit,
you have created this little living thing,
this pet,
as you have created me and
the entire world.

I know Father,
that you express your love,
your blessing
and your healing energy
through every living thing on this planet.

I know my God,
that your love is endless,
so right here and right now, I accept the
perfect and total healing and
blessing for this little pet.

With gratitude,
knowing and acceptance
I give thanks
and I affirm
AND SO IT IS!

Bear, p. 197.

HEALING THE PASSING OF EMILY OUR PET

She was my best friend.
She welcomed me when I came home,
And looked sad when I left.
She was grateful and loving
For everything I gave her.
She was my best friend.

Now she lays on vets table.
Thin, frail and lifeless.
I touch her.
Her body still warm,
But her little tongue does not lick my hand,
Nor does her tail wag with joy.

My eyes are laden with tears.
They create a curtain of glass
And my beautiful, loving Emily
Begins to fade from my vision.
My heart is heavy with grief
And my breathing is labored.

I close my eyes and turn inward.
How lucky I am.
How blessed I have been.
To have shared the love
Of this beautiful creation of God
For thirteen years.

This is the cycle of life.
These are the changes.
The sun rises and sets.
The new day is born
And the old one dies.
This is the cycle of life.

WAR

PEACE FROM WITHIN

One God.
One Mind.
One Globe
One People.

My mind soars
From place to place
From soul to soul.
Looking for peace.

Where is this peace?
Who holds the key?
I seek it!
Where do I find it?

I am lost and I hurt.
Pain is everywhere.
Quietly, I go within.
I search no more.

And as each of us
Finds the peace within
We become stronger.
We become peaceful.

And as this peace spreads
From one to another
We envelop the world
And we find God.

AGONY OF WAR

A flag-covered casket.
A blood-soaked uniform.
A mother's scream.

The loss of a son.
The flight of a soul.
The end of a human.

Testosterone gone wild
Inflated egos.
The wounded pride.

The leader's greed.
The peoples lack.
Man's sacrifice.

God's Creation.
Man's free will.
Creator's tears.

DEFENDERS OF FREEDOM

Beloved, defenders of freedom.
You are the veil,
Between good and evil.
You are defenders of justice
And keepers of peace.

How do we thank you
For putting yourselves on the line
To protect us and give our children future?
How do we say thank you
For risking *your* lives
For safety of *ours*?

We'll just look up to God and say
Please God, keep them safe and
Keep them in Your Holy Light.
O God, bring them home safely
And give **them** a future.

Made in the USA
San Bernardino, CA
04 October 2014